MAPPING THE EARTH

MAPPING EARTH'S HEMISPHERES

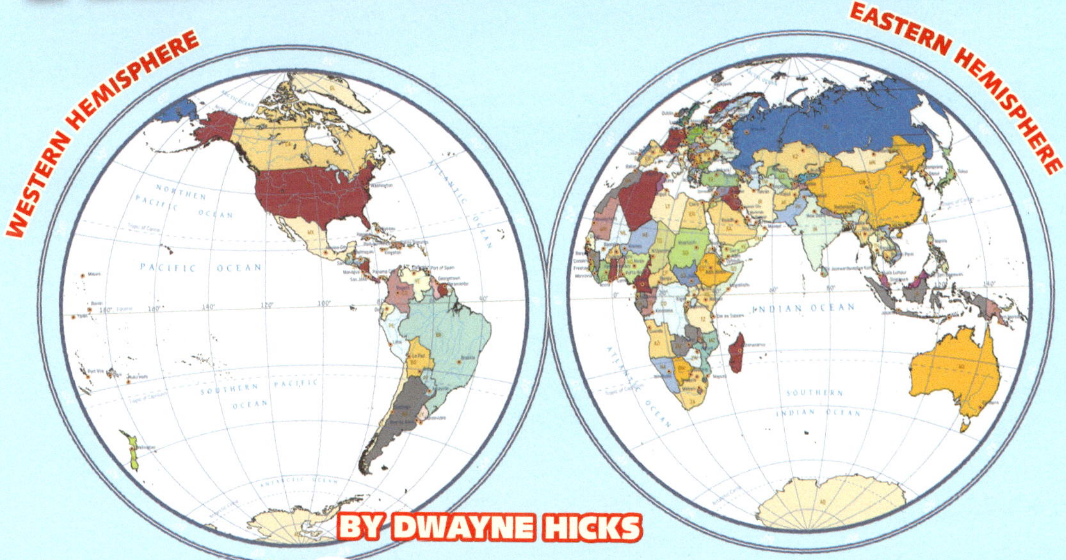

BY DWAYNE HICKS

Gareth Stevens PUBLISHING

Please visit our website, www.garethstevens.com. For a free color catalog of all our high-quality books, call toll free 1-800-542-2595 or fax 1-877-542-2596.

Library of Congress Cataloging-in-Publication Data

Names: Hicks, Dwayne, author.
Title: Mapping earth's hemispheres / Dwayne Hicks.
Description: New York : Gareth Stevens, 2023. | Series: Mapping the earth | Includes index.
Identifiers: LCCN 2021038537 (print) | LCCN 2021038538 (ebook) | ISBN 9781538278130 (library binding) | ISBN 9781538278116 (paperback) | ISBN 9781538278123 (6 pack) | ISBN 9781538278147 (ebook)
Subjects: LCSH: Atlases. | Northern hemisphere–Maps. | Southern Hemisphere–Maps. | Eastern Hemisphere–Maps. | Western hemisphere–Maps. | LCGFT: World atlases.
Classification: LCC G1021 .H693 2023 (print) | LCC G1021 (ebook) | DDC 912–dc23/eng/20211027
LC record available at https://lccn.loc.gov/2021038537
LC ebook record available at https://lccn.loc.gov/2021038538

Published in 2023 by
Gareth Stevens Publishing
29 E. 21st Street
New York, NY 10010

Portions of this work were originally authored by Todd Bluthenthal and published as *Earth's Hemispheres*. All new material in this edition was authored by Dwayne Hicks.

Designer: Tanya Dellaccio
Editor: Greg Roza

Photo credits: Cover Natalya_Konovalova/Shutterstock.com; pp. 2–24 (background texture) Triff/Shutterstock.com; p. 5 AJP/Shutterstock.com; p. 7 Soleil Nordic/Shutterstock.com; p. 9 BNP Design Studio/Shutterstock.com; pp. 11, 13, 15, 17, 19 (map) Peter Hermes Furian/Shutterstock.com; p. 13 TTstudio/Shutterstock.com; p. 15 Irina Sokolovskaya/Shutterstock.com; p. 17 ESB Professional/Shutterstock.com; p. 19 Thiago Leite/Shutterstock.com; p. 21 Bonnie Fink/Shutterstock.com.

Printed in the United States of America

CPSIA compliance information: Batch #CSGS23. For further information contact Gareth Stevens, New York, New York at 1-800-542-2595.

CONTENTS

Boldface words appear in the glossary.

Around the Globe

A globe is a ball-shaped map of Earth! There are lines on most globes that **divide** Earth into hemispheres. A hemisphere is half of the globe. "Hemi" means "half." "Sphere" is another word for "globe."

Imaginary Lines

People have long used **imaginary** lines to show Earth's hemispheres. Latitude lines show how far north or south a place is. They run east and west. Longitude lines show how far east or west a place is. They run north and south.

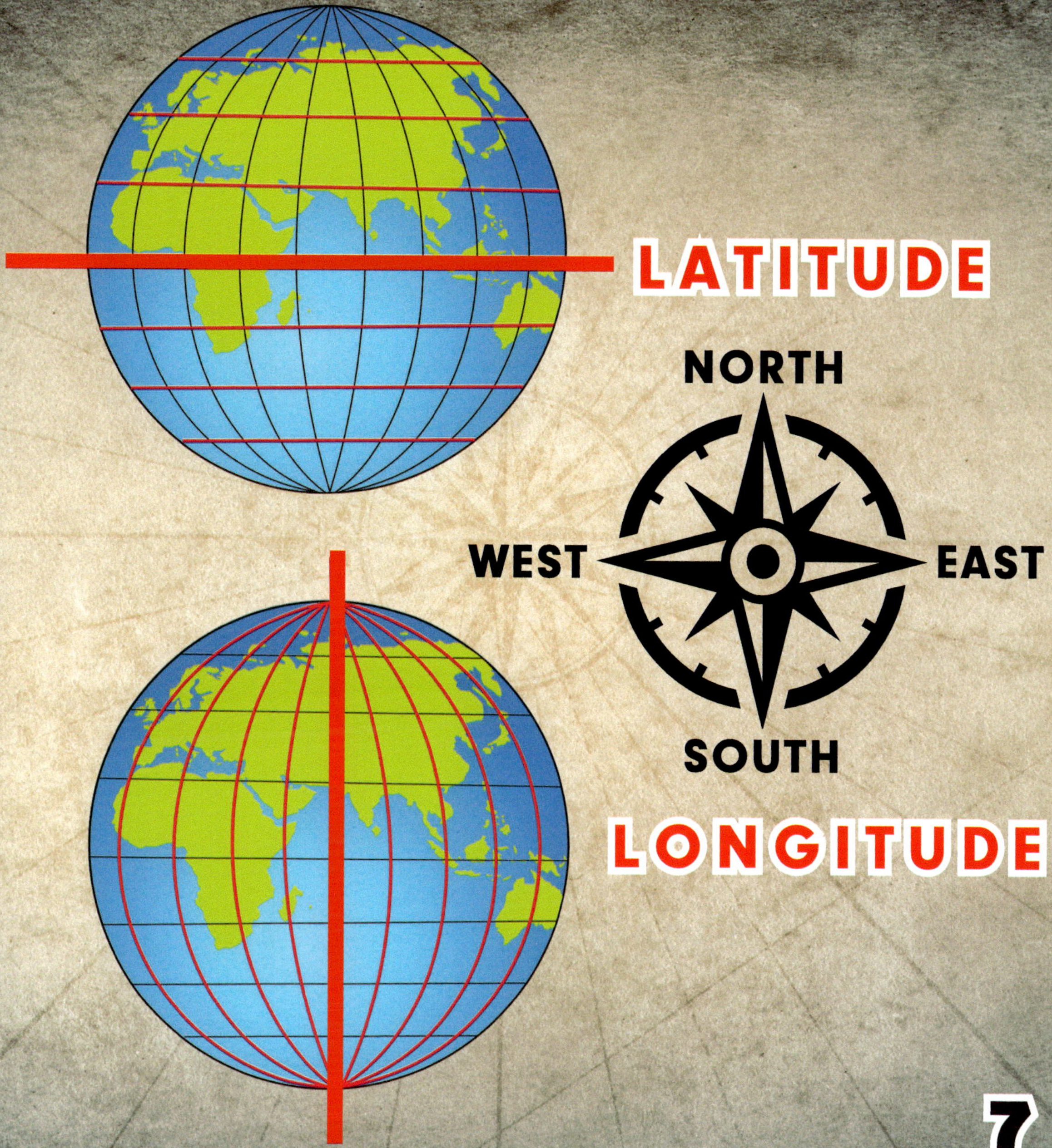
LATITUDE
NORTH
WEST
EAST
SOUTH
LONGITUDE

Four Hemispheres

Lines of latitude and longitude show where two hemispheres meet. Earth has four hemispheres because it can be **split** in half two ways. They are the Northern Hemisphere, the Southern Hemisphere, the Western Hemisphere, and the Eastern Hemisphere.

NORTHERN HEMISPHERE
SOUTHERN HEMISPHERE

WESTERN HEMISPHERE
EASTERN HEMISPHERE

Dividing Earth

The equator is the main line of latitude running east and west. This imaginary line divides the Northern and Southern Hemispheres. The prime meridian is the main line of longitude running north and south. It divides the Eastern and Western Hemispheres.

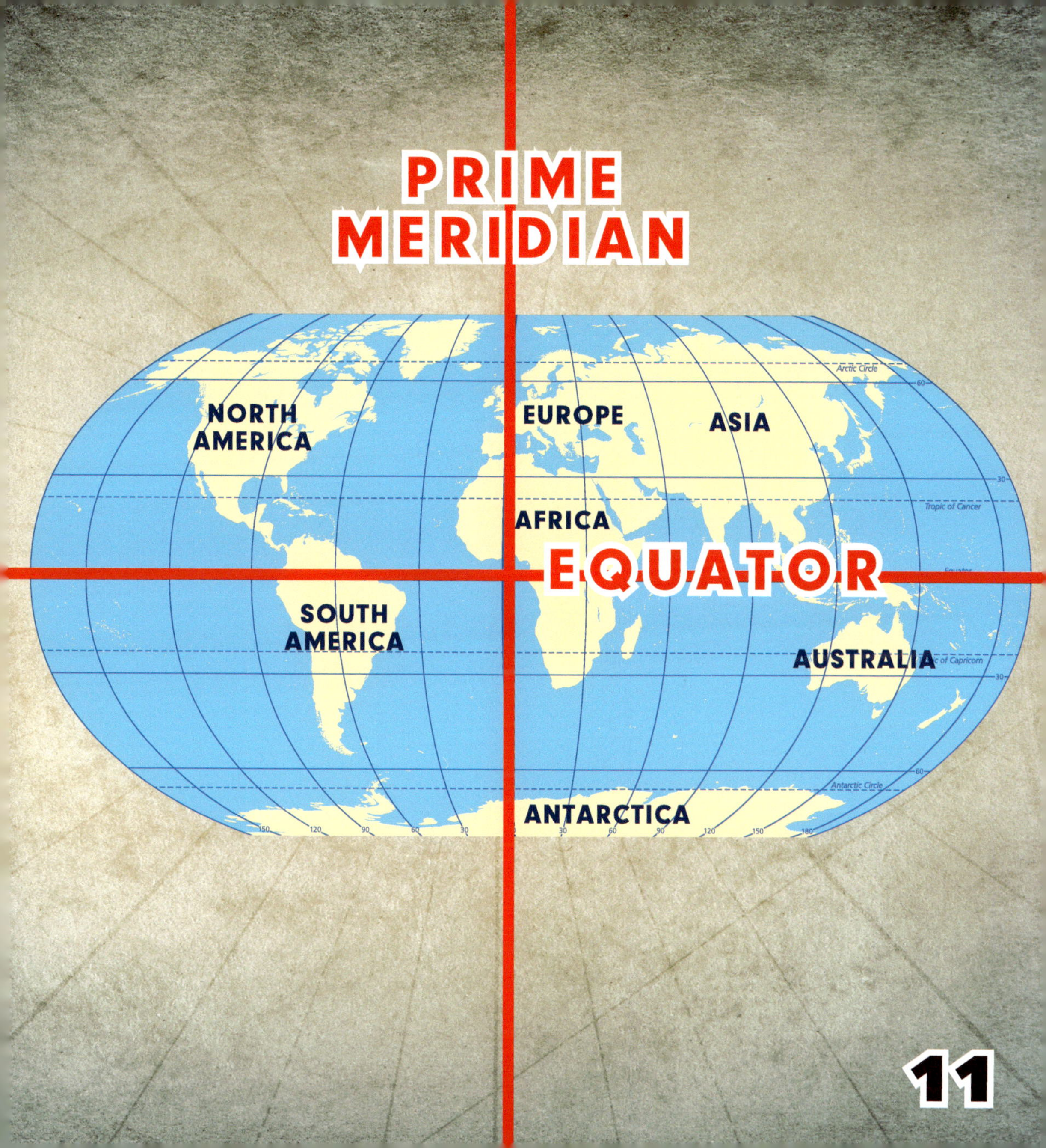
PRIME
MERIDIAN
NORTH
AMERICA
EUROPE
ASIA
Arctic Circle
Tropic of Cancer
AFRICA
EQUATOR
SOUTH
AMERICA
AUSTRALIA
Antarctic Circle
ANTARCTICA

Up North

The Northern Hemisphere is the half of Earth north of the equator. Almost 90 **percent** of Earth's **population** live in the Northern Hemisphere! That's because almost all of Earth's land is north of the equator.

NORTHERN HEMISPHERE
EQUATOR
NEW YORK, NEW YORK

Down South

The Southern Hemisphere is south of the equator. Australia and Antarctica are the only **continents** in the Southern Hemisphere. Most of South America is too. The oceans in the Southern Hemisphere are larger than the oceans in the Northern Hemisphere.

SYDNEY, AUSTRALIA

In the East

The Eastern Hemisphere is east of the prime meridian. The Eastern Hemisphere has about two-thirds of Earth's land. More than 80 percent of the people in the world live in the Eastern Hemisphere. About 4.56 **billion** people live in Asia alone!

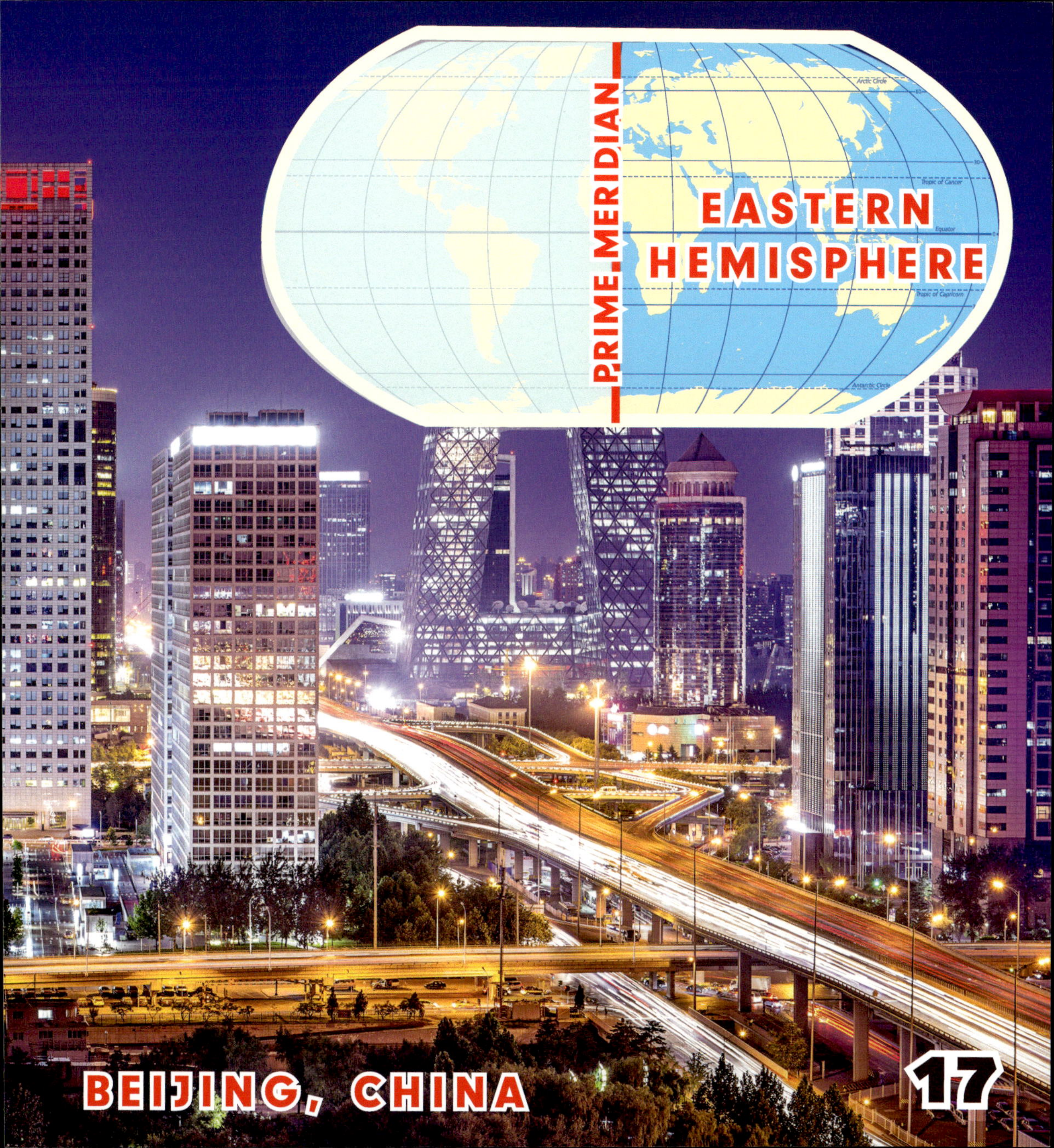
PRIME MERIDIAN
EASTERN HEMISPHERE
Arctic Circle
Tropic of Cancer
Equator
Tropic of Capricorn
Antarctic Circle
BEIJING, CHINA

In the West

The Western Hemisphere is west of the prime meridian. All of North America and South America are located in the Western Hemisphere. Most of the Pacific Ocean and Atlantic Ocean are in this hemisphere.

SÃO PAULO, BRAZIL

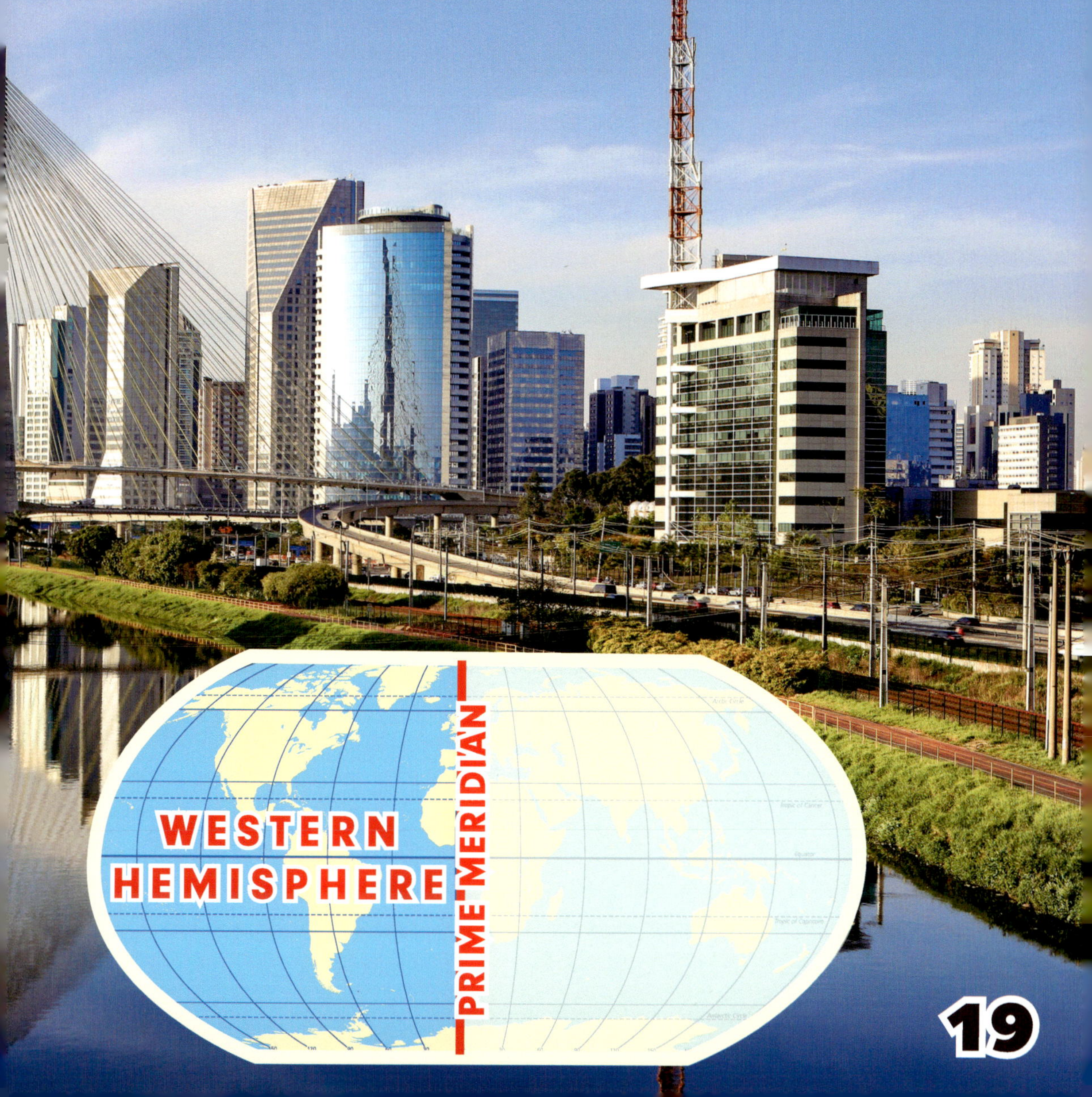

Where Is Everyone?

Most people on Earth live in the Northern Hemisphere. That's because almost all of Earth's land is north of the equator. Almost no one lives in Antarctica in the Southern Hemisphere. It's far too cold and windy there!

ANTARCTICA,
SOUTHERN HEMISPHERE

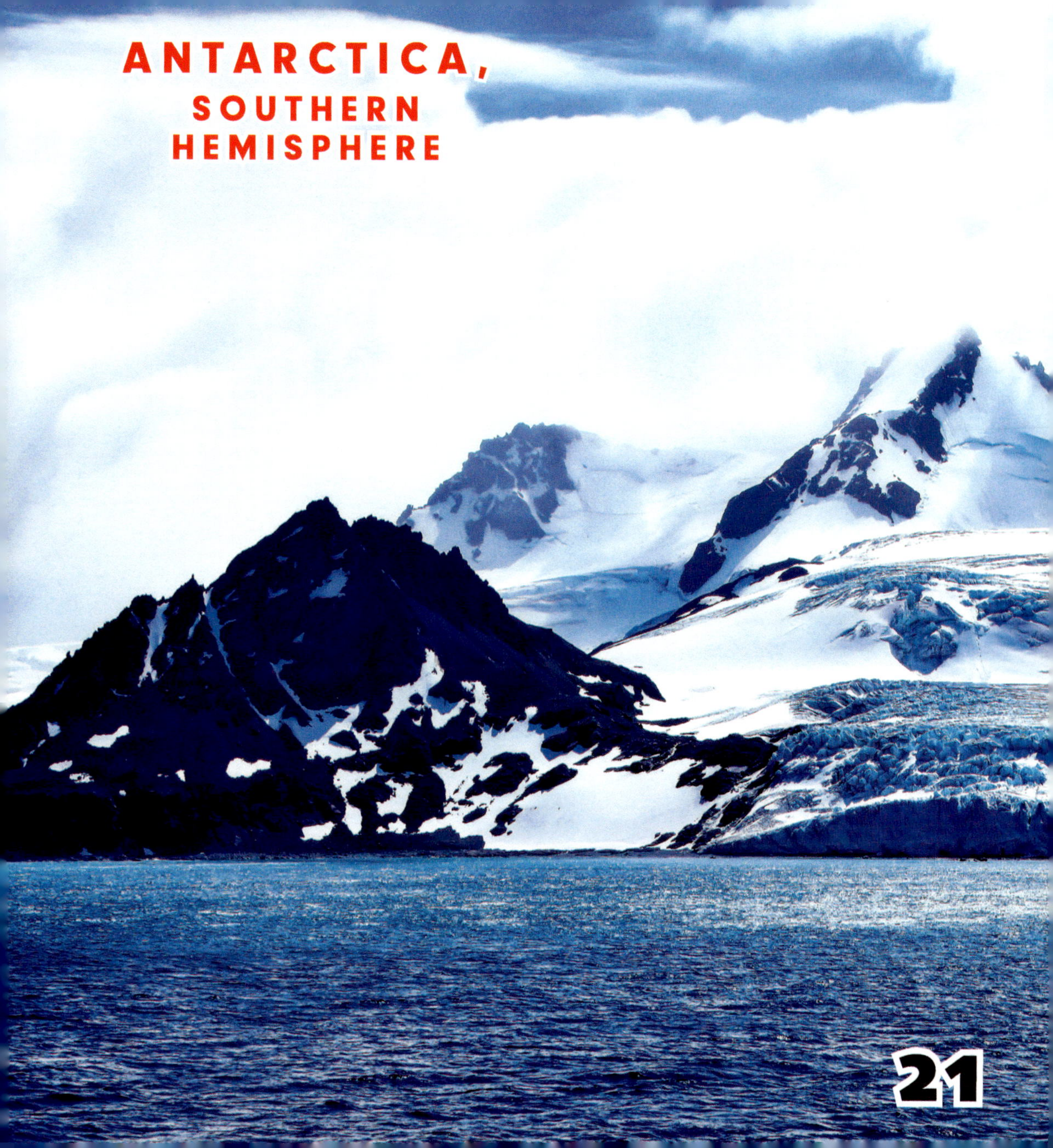

GLOSSARY

billion: a thousand millions, or 1,000,000,000

continent: one of Earth's seven great landmasses

divide: to break up

imaginary: not real, or existing only in the mind

percent: a small part of a whole

population: the number of people who live in an area

split: broken apart

FOR MORE INFORMATION

BOOKS

Esbaum, Jill. *National Geographic Little Kids First Big Book of Where*. Washington, D.C.: National Geographic Kids, 2020.

Gallion, Sue Lowell. *Our World: A First Book of Geography*. London, UK: Phaidon Press, 2020.

National Kids. *My First Atlas of the World*. Washington, D.C.: National Geographic Kids, 2018.

WEBSITES

Ducksters: Geography
www.ducksters.com/geography/
This age-friendly site provides a wealth of information about Earth's geography. It includes maps.

Hemisphere
kids.britannica.com/kids/article/hemisphere/346139
Learn more about Earth's four hemispheres.

INDEX